To Jack Bedford Barnard

ISBN 0-590-33028-4

Text copyright © 1996 by Tanis Jordan.
Illustrations copyright © 1996 by Martin Jordan.
All rights reserved. Published by Scholastic Inc., 555 Broadway,
New York, NY 10012, by arrangement with
Larousse Kingfisher Chambers Inc.

12 11 10 9 8 7 6 5 4 3 2 1   7 8 9/9 0 1 2/0

Printed in the U.S.A.   08

First Scholastic printing, March 1997

Designed by Caroline Johnson.

Amazon Alphabet

Martin and Tanis Jordan

SCHOLASTIC INC.
New York Toronto London Auckland Sydney

Aa
is for
Agouti
eating Brazil nuts

"A-*goo*-tee"

Bb
is for
Butterfly
fluttering by

Cc *is for* Caiman

drowsing in the sun

"*Kay-mun*"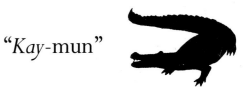

Dd *is for* Dolphin

diving for fish

E e *is for* Eagle

ready to swoop

Ff

is for

Frog

leaping from a leaf

Gg *is for*
Giant Armadillo
snuffling for ants

Hh

is for

Hummingbird

sipping nectar from a flower

Ii *is for* Iguana
watchful and still

"Ig-wah-na"

Jj

is for

Jaguar

preparing to prowl

Kk

is for

Kinkajou

hanging by its tail

"King-ka-joo"

Ll *is for* Leaf-nosed Bat

chasing a moth

Mm *is for* Macaw

nibbling a wild fruit

"Muh-*kaw*"

Nn *is for*

Night Monkey

waking at dusk

Oo

is for

Ocelot

protecting its kittens

"*Oss-uh-lot*"

Pp *is for* Piranha

snapping its teeth

 "Pih-*rah*-na"

Qq *is for* Quetzal

perching to eat

Rr

is for

Red Ouakari

leaping through trees

"Woh-*kah*-ree"

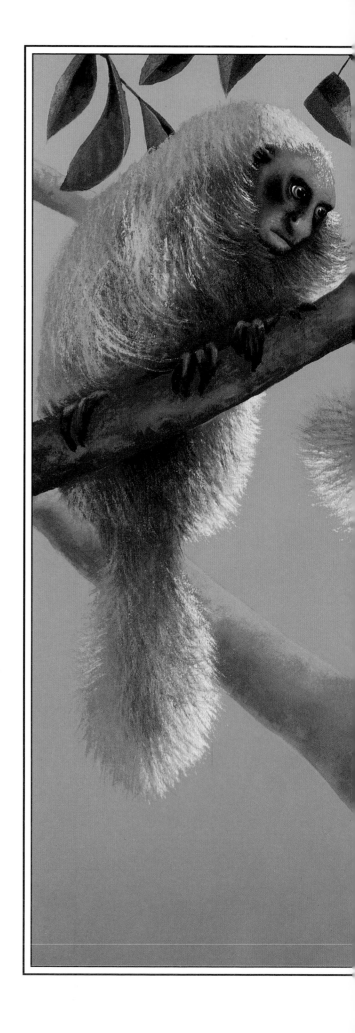

Ss

is for
Sloth

grooming its coat

Tt
is for
Toucan
with its raucous call

"Too-can"

Uu *is for* Umbrella Bird

with a bright red wattle

V v *is for* Vine Snake

on a cannonball tree

"Peck-a-ree"

Ww *is for*
White-collared Peccary
that lives in a herd

Xx *is for* X-ray Fish

swimming past the weeds

"Ya-pock"

Y y *is for* Yapok

stalking a fish

Zz is for Zorro

hidden in the tree,
the last amazing animal
in this Amazon ABC

"Zor-oh"

NOTES

A
Agouti (A-*goo*-tee) *mammal*
The agouti is a rodent about the size of a rabbit. It feeds on fallen fruits, nuts, and seeds and lives in an underground burrow. Agoutis bury Brazil nuts to eat later, but often they do not return for them and these nuts grow into Brazil nut trees.

B

Butterfly *insect*
The Amazon has some of the biggest and most brilliant butterflies in the world. Some fly in swarms so large that they can be seen from airplanes. The large butterfly is called a Marpesia. The little butterfly is called an "eighty-eight" because the markings on its wings are like the figure 88.

C

Caiman (*Kay*-mun) *reptile*
Caimans are South American alligators. Some grow up to 6 feet long and can live for more than 50 years. Caimans need to breathe air, so they swim with the tips of their snouts out of the water. They often keep their mouths open when resting.

D

Dolphin *mammal*
All dolphins are mammals and need to breathe air. Amazon River dolphins are freshwater animals and cannot survive in the sea. Pinker in color than their saltwater relatives, river dolphins are major predators in Amazonian rivers, feeding on fish.

E

Eagle *bird*
Harpy eagles are the largest of all eagles. They make nests in the tops of tall trees and swoop down to hunt monkeys, sloths, agoutis, and yapoks. They can even fly upside down beneath the crowns of the trees to pluck prey from the branches.

F
Frog *amphibian*
The Latin name for this species of frog is *Hyla favosa*. It is a tree frog and has suction pads on its toes to help it grip branches and leaves. Tree frogs are active at night and during the day. They feed on insects by jumping up and seizing them in the air.

G

Giant Armadillo *mammal*
Giant armadillos grow up to 5 feet long and can weigh more than 100 pounds. They eat spiders, snakes, certain plants, and insects. Using their powerful sense of smell, armadillos sniff out ant and termite nests, breaking them open with the massive claws on their front feet to reach insects inside.

H
Hummingbird *bird*
Hummingbirds beat their wings rapidly as they hover, producing the hum that gives them their name. The frilled coquette hummingbird also buzzes like a bee, and defends its territory aggressively.

I
Iguana (Ig-*wah*-na) *reptile*
Green iguanas can grow to 6 feet long. Iguanas are cold-blooded and climb to the tops of trees to warm themselves in the early morning sun. If threatened, an iguana will drop straight out of a tree onto the forest floor or into a river to escape.

Jaguar *mammal*
With a body up to 6 feet long, the jaguar is the largest cat in South America. It lies in wait for its prey on low, thick branches and drops straight onto the back of a peccary, deer, or tapir that comes within range. The jaguar is the only big cat that doesn't roar.

Kinkajou (*King***-ka-joo)** *mammal*
The kinkajou spends all its time in the trees. It uses its strong, long tail to grip, but it does not leap from branch to branch. Instead, it curls its tail around branches and hangs down, leaving its "hands" free to reach fruits or break open bees' nests for honey.

Leaf-nosed Bat *mammal*
This leaf-nosed bat feeds on moths and other insects which it catches in flight. No one knows exactly how many species of leaf-nosed bat live in the Amazon. Some species eat frogs, birds, and lizards. Others prefer nectar from flowers.

Macaw (*Muh***-*kaw***) *bird***
Hyacinth macaws eat fruit, seeds, nuts, and leaves, and are 3 feet long from head to tail. They are the largest flying parrots in the world. Macaws use their strong beaks to break open Brazil nut pods to eat the nuts inside. They nest in holes in trees.

Night Monkey *mammal*
Night monkeys are the only monkeys in the Amazon that are active at night. They emerge from their treeholes at a precise time—15 minutes after sunset—to search for fruit and to catch flying insects.

Ocelot (*Oss***-uh-lot)** *mammal*
The ocelot is a small cat, about 3 feet long. An ocelot has between two and four kittens, and they usually stay with their mother until she has taught them to hunt for themselves. Ocelots have exceptional eyesight and hearing, and very sensitive whiskers, which they use when hunting.

Piranha (Pih-*rah***-na)** *fish*
The red-bellied piranha is one of nearly 20 species of piranha that live in Amazonian rivers. Piranhas have sharp teeth and jaws powerful enough to bite through steel wire. They hunt in shoals of 10 to 100.

Quetzal (*Ket***-sal)** *bird*
The Amazonian Pavonine quetzal has a shorter tail than other species of quetzal. Living in dense parts of the Amazon forest it feeds on insects and small fruits. Quetzals nest in rotting wood or empty wasps' nests.

Red Ouakari (Wok-*ah***-ree)** *mammal*
The red ouakari, sometimes known as the bald ouakari, is very agile, leaping from tree to tree in search of fruit, leaves, buds, and seeds to eat. In the wild its face is bright red but if the animal is kept in captivity, the red color fades.

Sloth *mammal*

The three-toed sloth feeds mainly on cecropia (si-*croh*-pee-ah) leaves. Some sloths stay in the same tree for years, sleeping up to 18 hours a day. Sloths move so slowly that a plant called algae grows in their fur and camouflages them in the trees.

Toucan (*Too*-can) *bird*

The keel-billed toucan's call is a harsh, rasping sound. Its massive bill is sharp and strong but surprisingly light. Toucans roost in holes in trees, tucking their bills under their wings when they sleep. They feed on fruit and berries.

Umbrella Bird *bird*

Umbrella birds have glossy, feathered crests on their heads. The male also has a large red air sac called a wattle hanging from his throat with a single feather on its tip. The female has a small and less significant wattle. The male inflates his wattle to make a booming, hooting call.

Vine Snake *reptile*

When vine snakes hang motionless in the trees, they look like jungle lianas or vines. Unlike most snakes, vine snakes do not glide smoothly but move jerkily like falling vegetation. Vine snakes are slender and grow up to 4 feet long. They are poisonous and eat mostly lizards.

White-collared Peccary (*Peck*-a-ree) *mammal*

White-collared peccaries live in herds of up to 50, traveling through the forest and foraging in the leaves for plants and roots. They have sharp tusks to defend themselves when necessary. One adult male makes a sound like a cough to call the herd together.

X-ray Fish *fish*

X-ray fish are daring when in big shoals, but in small groups they are shy and stay in shady places or among water plants. They are almost transparent. X-ray fish are tiny and grow to only about 2 inches long.

Yapok (*Ya*-pock) *mammal*

Yapoks are water opossums and live along the river bank. They have webbed feet and sensitive whiskers which they use to detect movements in the water. Female yapoks carry their young in pouches in their abdomens. Even when they dive deep into the river the young stay safe.

Zorro (*Zor*-oh) *mammal*

Zorro is the Spanish word for fox but the zorro is really the largest of the South American wild dogs. Little is known about this mysterious animal, reminding us that much remains to be discovered about Amazon wildlife.